Shameless Self-Promotion:
Antics and Lessons From a First Year Vlogger

Megan Gotham

4

Copyright © 2012
Megan Gotham
All Rights Reserved.

Cover photo copyright 2009
John Walker Photography
All Rights Reserved.

ISBN-13: 978-1468181326

ISBN-10: 1468181327

No part of this book may be reproduced, in part or in whole, in any manor, without the expressed written consent of the copyright holder.

Disclaimer:
 The stories and events described in this book are based on the real life experiences of the author. Slight details and names may be changed to protect third party identities. Any likeness or association to any other person, living or dead, real or fictional, is purely coincidental.

6

Dedicated to my partner in crime,
Dannielle Johnson
(aka Dannielle Johnson-Isaac, to which I add
the hyphenated last name begrudgingly).

Haha - I just told the entire world your real name!

Table of Contents:

Side Note:	**10**
Introduction	**11**
Shameless Self-Promotion is an Art Form	**13**
What to Vlog About?	**20**
User Name = Happy User	**25**
Don't Forget, You Still Have a Face!	**31**
Be a (Vlog) Whore	**33**
Viewers Only See What You Allow Them to See	**38**
EDIT!	**41**
Rule #1: Don't Anger the Gods of Advertising!	**46**
You Can be Sabotaged!	**58**
Copyrights Run Both Ways	**64**

Be You... But More Interesting	69
Be Interesting, Not Ashamed	72
Inconsistency = Haters. Consistency = Haters.	77
When in Doubt; Fake It!	83
Don't Vlog with Friends!	86
Social Media is Your BFF	93
Who Do You Vlog For?	97
Ending Thoughts	99

Side Note:

The following, pamphlet-sized, book is not a how-to or get-rich-quick guide. It is a series of thoughts, personal experiences, and advice written by a vlogger, with the hopes of helping other vloggers find their groove. As such, the terminology used within this book assumes that those reading it are already familiar with the general vlogging vernacular. If you should have any problems understanding a phrase in this book, please use an Internet search engine, as a standard dictionary will be of no use to you.

Introduction

Who doesn't want to work from home and make a legitimate living? How about a job where you can do and say whatever you want? That's the dream of being a professional blog writer or vlogger (short for video blogger).

Imagine, millions of fans and followers hanging onto your every word. There would be no boss to please, or terrible hours to fulfill; you never even have to leave the house if you don't want to. Heck, you'll make so much money sharing your thoughts that you could pay someone to be your personal shopper anyways!

Now stop imagining where a vlog or blog could take you, and realize this simple truth: it is just as easy to abandon a vlog as it is to start one. If owning a webcam or having thoughts on a subject could make everyone rich, than everyone in the world would be rich from vlogging, wouldn't they? Before you put yourself out there, on the Internet, with the intention of making a living, there are many things that you should consider first.

Shameless Self-Promotion

is an Art Form

Shameless self-promotion, aka advertising yourself to anyone, anywhere, any time, is a common way to show the word that you exist. While a new vlogger can be tempted to whore their name all over the Internet, this is not likely to boost their viewership. Sure, you may get a few hits here or there, but it's unlikely that your videos will "catch on" through self-advertising online. To the contrary, having your fans organically pass your videos around will usually do more than all of the promotional tricks in the world combined. Because of this, it can be a slow and daunting process to get any attention as a vlogger; but at least you can be confident in knowing that the viewership you do receive is sincere.

Believe me, subscription services, advertisements, and other sources of getting your name out there can become very tempting. At one point, I had decided to do a vlog about my favorite vloggers. My intention was to gush over their videos, as if to present myself as a rabid fangirl, then tag the vloggers' usernames so that my video would appear in their search results. All of this was done with the hope of snagging a few people here and there for my own vlog. It's not an uncommon tactic for newer, or more desperate, vloggers, but then a thought came to me:

I truly did like those vloggers, so what if posting this video and tagging them presented itself as a cheap trick (which it was), and that, in turn, got me on my favorite vloggers' bad sides? In fact, the more I sat with the idea, the more I hated it. It no longer made sense to try to gain subscribers by muscling in on someone else's spotlight. I wanted to be better than that.

All the same, though, I had already recorded the video, and so I decided to post it without tags. At least that way, it was free advertising to my favorite vloggers, instead of me acting like an attention whore. The result actually stunned me.

I logged into my account the next day to find a new comment in my inbox. Somehow, even without a tag, one of my favorite vloggers, XiaoRishu, had found my video praising her channel. She left me a simple "<3" comment, which made my own heart soar. Even with thousands of subscribers, she had managed to find my video, hours after it was posted, and took the time out of her day to leave a comment. That, for me, was more encouraging that a thousand "thumbs up" clicks, or a million subscribers.

The moral of my story is to not worry about running the rat race of finding fans. Just do things in your own way and let your followers build in their own time. Whether you have an audience of billions, or just a handful of viewers, you have to be patient enough to let things happen naturally, and at their own pace.

Being authentically you, and using your time to produce quality videos, will be more effective than trying too hard to advertise your vlog for the sake of attempting to force an audience to love you, or your products, as the case may be. You may believe that having viewers or subscribers will aid you in a revenue sharing get-rich-quick scheme, or that you truly have something great to offer in your videos, but, you cannot force people to watch. The truth is that expensive advertising campaigns can easily wear you out emotionally, kill your motivation to make vlogs, and quickly drain all of your funding.

Even though most people start out with the thought that they'll never need a paid advertisement for their vlog, many change their minds. After you have worn your fingers to the bone, with no results, you may easily feel desperate enough to turn to paid marketing tactics. This is where things get tricky, because the market to promote yourself in is endless, yet your financial resources should be extremely finite. The old adage, "you have to spend money to make money," does not necessarily apply to vlogging. You can spend eight million dollars advertising your vlog and never make even a fraction of your money back.

I rather prefer the phrase, "if you build it, they will come." The idea is to create unique, entertaining videos that people flock to. You have to be patient and hone your craft of creating interesting vlogs, and then, if you're diligent, and a little bit lucky, your audience will find you –

free of charge.

What to Vlog About?

The first, and most important, aspect of vlogging is to figure out what exactly you want to talk about. This is something that may take days, or even years, to figure out. That doesn't mean that you can't vlog about random topics in the meantime, though!

As for myself, I started vlogging because I was down in the dumps. I had a business venture go sour, I was relocated with the military and had an extremely difficult time making friends, and I was feeling depressed – so I got up one day and did something about it. I couldn't afford therapy (I couldn't even afford the co-pay to get dental work done!), so I turned on my camera and started talking about myself instead.

I had been inspired by other vloggers, like Kandee Johnson, and wanted to portray a squeaky clean image, hoping that people would love and adore me. It took quite a few months before I felt more comfortable in my own vlogging skin. I started to allow myself to complain, rant, and even curse as my personal wall began falling down.

Surprisingly, that attracted more followers than anything else I had attempted to do. I suppose the idea of a perfect, happy homemaker was less tolerable than the angrier version of myself, who was fed up with the other military wives (who were always running their mouths). Being "real" got me more attention and respect than trying to be perfect, and so that became more of my vlogging angle than anything.

Just remember, if you begin a vlog with no strategy or plan for where you want it to go, it can end up anywhere, just like your life. I felt that I had too many ideas and interests to limit myself to one topic or field, so, I narcissistically called my vlog "Megan Vlog: Weird, Random, Wonderful!" I had everything from tutorials to screaming rants on parenting. The only downside was that some people didn't care for the diversity of my videos, which has likely lost me quite a few followers.

Before *you* start a vlog though, you may find that you would be more successful with a single topic. As an example, if you are a computer guru, that may be the only category that you want to vlog about. If you want to produce parenting videos, that may also be a singular area. But, if you want to make educational ABC cartoons, interlaced with videos of you venting and swearing, you will likely be met with a lot of anger and confusion from the masses. This is a normal reaction, as audiences tend to prefer one-dimensional public figures that they can easily predict.

Similarly, you will have a much easier time finding your audience if you focus on a need. For instance, tutorials, how-tos, advice, and so forth tend to attract the most subscribers. If you instead want to speak about your personal life, you're videos will not likely appear as readily in general searches. You'll also tend to warrant less interest from any viewers who do not know you personally.

Many popular vloggers started off with tutorials, and then began to make personal videos as their viewership grew. Their audience's reactions are often mixed, as some people like to watch stories about their favorite vloggers children or personal day, and others only want the vloggers to post more tutorials that are helpful and relevant. Nevertheless, the personal posts are still viewed by thousands of people.

User Name = Happy User

Just like superheroes, vloggers can also hide safely behind a secret identity. If you have ever followed a vlog, you have probably noticed that most of the vloggers only give out a limited amount of their personal information. This is no accident. Many vloggers have handed out their full names, only to find themselves being cyber stalked, by fans and haters alike.

Consider this: if you have a personal profile on any social media website, and you vlog using your full name, anyone will have the ability to look you up. If you include your phone number, address, or other sensitive information on your profile, that is now in the hands of random strangers. Even if you don't have that information listed, or your profile is private, there are many online services that charge a small fee to hand out your personal, and even unlisted, details. This, in turn, opens you up to types of harassment that you could never fathom.

If you tell people the name of the city that you live in, someday, someone may find out where your house is, and then you risk having a real-life stalker. Now ponder what would happen if this stalker isn't a fan, but hates you with a passion instead. It may sound extreme, but, the more you express an opinion online, the more you will hear everyone's counter-opinion, and if you irritate the wrong person, purposefully or not, there's no telling what he/she might do if given the opportunity.

Several years ago, a news story came on about a woman in the same city that I was residing in. She had listed puppies for sale on a local classified add site. Apparently, the woman had no phone, so she listed her address instead. This resulted in some random stranger showing up at her front door and shooting her in the face!

To put the matter bluntly, it's better to be on the paranoid, and safe, side rather then take a risk of leaking your personal information to the entire Internet, then regretting it later. Once someone has your information, you can never get it back, even if you remove the vlog posts. So, to avoid the potential hassle of having to change your email address, phone number, or even be forced to move, you should keep your privacy a priority.

When I first began blogging publicly, I made up a pseudonym. For several years I was Brittany Sloan, a blogger for a non-profit organization. Being Brittany was great, because, I made up an email address, allowed readers to contact me there, and I could be as connected, or as distant, to my followers as I chose to be.

If someone hated me, I could block that person from contacting me again. There were times when someone disliked me so much, that, even after blocking them, they would log into another email address and harass me further. When this happened, and it inevitably does to every professional blogger, I was grateful that I used a fake name. Because of that, I did not have to worry that some psycho would look up my address and send me anthrax in the mail, or show up at my front door when I have small children at home.

My personal advice to all of you is to sincerely weigh out the pros and cons of using your real name online. Consider this as well: you may have no worries about people knowing who you are today, but what if you vlog for years, and, someday, you have a career and a family to worry about? Or, perhaps you stop vlogging, but leave the videos online; in which case, they could rub someone the wrong way at any point in time (and some people are just looking for someone to hate, whether you said anything offensive or not). Do you want the potential risk of putting your kids or job at stake because a random nobody decides that they want to fixate on destroying your life? Throwing someone off of your trail by giving them a full, but fake, name offers you much more personal protection as a whole.

I've heard the argument that, by using a fake name, "Hollywood people" can't find you. To this I say: almost no one moves from independent vlogging into the entertainment industry. Justin Bieber was an oddity. If someone does contact you with a record or movie deal, be careful, because it's more than likely a scam to lure you out and kidnap, rape, sell, or kill you. Thousands of young people disappear every year – be smart!

Don't Forget, You Still Have a Face!

My BFF, Quinn, had an embarrassing experience as a new vlogger. She used a fake name, but tagged her small hometown in her videos. Since the people she knew never mentioned her vlog, she assumed that her posts were safely concealed from their eyes, and so she began to vent in her videos about people she knew locally (especially her ex-husband).

One day, her ex showed up at her front door and angrily stated that he had been emailed her vlogs from one of his friends. This kicked up an extreme amount of drama between the two. Quinn had never used her name, or her ex's name, but, the other people in town knew her face and voice, so they knew who she was talking about. This can happen to you too!

Never think that you are safe or protected as a vlogger. Once something is publicly posted online it is out there for everyone to find, and, believe me, they always find it eventually. In that respect, be overly cautious, not only in what you say, but how you tag yourself. It is amazing just how fast people find out exactly what you have said about them.

Be a (Vlog) Whore

Perhaps the best part about independent vlogging is that there are no set rules. You are allowed to be as fluid as water with the topics that you decide to vlog about. There are downsides to this freedom, though.

Maybe you want to do nothing but make-up tutorials on your channel, but then you find that you are unable to get noticed due to the extremely high number of cosmetic related vlogs that are already out there. It's then up to you to chose whether to spice up your current posts, turn to advertising, or change what you vlog about. As vloggers, we must adapt, or else we die out.

Now, what does that mean?

Basically, it means that if you aren't finding your audience, change things around until you do. You're the boss of your vlog, and so, no one but you can decide what to post. That means it's okay to experiment and try everything under the sun while on a quest to find your audience.

When I started vlogging for myself (versus blogging for an organization, as mentioned previously), I could not pick a topic to focus on. This was similar to the problem in my day-to-day life, where I had so many interests that I could never pick a career field to enter into. I don't like to pinhole myself into a single topic, because I consider myself to be too multi-dimensional for that.

As an example: one of my first videos started collecting a lot of hits (several thousand), while all of my other videos had an average of ten views at that point. The video receiving all of this attention was a how-to crafting video using ribbons, and, so, several websites about crafts were passing that single vlog post around. This gave me free advertising, and, while it wasn't gaining me any new subscribers, it still gave me hope as to how easily my vlog could snowball into something grand.

Normally, if I find a topic that "works," meaning it gains my vlog a lot of attention, I will run it into the ground, making sure to exploit the subject as much as possible before letting it go. Unfortunately, that was one of the only crafting videos I ever recorded, simply due to the fact that I had no other ideas for similar vlogs. Instead, I kept going with random videos, picking topics based on trial and error. If I had been more craft-competent, I may have chosen that as the only subject used in my vlog from that day on.

Nonetheless, I'm quite content with the randomness of my vlog and how it has shaped itself over the past year. I can talk about everything, from zombies, to pets, to military life. Sometimes it attracts new fans, because I'm so diverse; other times, it alienates viewers who only want to see rants on sorority recruitment, but who have no interest in hearing about anything else that I have to say. It's a gamble to run a vlog about random topics, but it's also quite fulfilling.

My lesson then, to pass on to all of you, is to never stop trying. The term "attention whore" doesn't sound flattering, but, in reality, it has allowed me to do and say whatever I want, whenever I want, without having to worry about fitting into a particular niche. If you have a single topic that works for you right from the start, then pursue that for as long as you desire, but never be afraid to mix it up, throw in random posts or personal entries, and/or to try something new. It may very well be those "weird" videos that make you stand out from the other vloggers.

Viewers Only See What You Allow Them to See

I, honestly, cannot tell you enough how wonderful this fact is! Once you stop filming, there's no way for anyone to ever know what was really going on off screen (unless you write a book about it later, of course...). If you flip over in your chair, you can remove that part. If there's a stack of dirty dished behind the camera, no one will know. Heck, there might be a Leprechaun behind you that refuses to move, and you can simply position yourself to hide the magic man on film. What isn't on camera is a mystery, and, typically, the viewers never think about what isn't seen. Perception is reality, especially when recording.

Most of my videos depict me, in a clean room, well dressed, with full make-up. However, 99.99% of the time, I was vlogging with no intention to leave the house that day, so, I often wore a nice, dressy top, and paired it with pajama pants – if I wore pants at all! But you'd never know that by watching the videos, because I sit behind my desk when I record a vlog.

And, unless you are a particularly fancy vlogger who uses many different takes and camera angles, it's fairly easy to create an impression on screen that may be false. There have been so many times where my husband would throw his armor on the floor, right in my recording zone, and I would have no way to move these heavy pieces of equipment. So, I would just sit a particular way so that the camera would block the giant piles of junk located behind me. By doing this, my room appeared neat and tidy on film, when it was much less flattering in person.

EDIT!

You may think that you are the most charismatic person on the planet, or some kind of one-take wonder, but, sooner or later, you are going to mess up and need to edit a recording. The good news: most computers come with some type of free video editing software. The bad news: you need to actually sit down and watch the entire recording to do a decent edit. If your video is only a few minutes long, then that's not a problem, but if you ramble for an hour or more, the editing process can be challenging, and boring.

When I first began vlogging, I didn't feel the need to edit. I would leave in my silent pauses, confused looks (when I forgot where I was going with a topic), and even my frequent uses of "uhh" and "umm." Those videos didn't get many hits, and rightfully so.

After about six months of vlogging, I decided to vent about a group of people who had been under my skin – snotty, mean military wives. I ranted, raved, and even swore for the first time in any of my vlog posts. I then rewatched the film and wasn't happy with the whole take. All of those pauses and constantly saying "umm" suddenly didn't seem appealing any longer. In fact, it made me look more than a little dumb to go from angry to looking confused within seconds. So, I opened up an editing program and cut out everything that wasn't a part of my rant. I didn't even allow myself enough space to breath in my finished product; as soon as one word ended, another was beginning. I call this rapid editing, without knowing the true and proper terminology.

This video became my first vlog to ever be shared by individuals. This time, a website wasn't passing one of my vlogs around, but actual people were sharing it on their social networking profiles. At that point, I decided to continue with rapid editing, which has helped to exponentially raise my viewership in all of my videos.

What this has taught me is that the audience has a short attention span, and if you can't get to the point fast enough, they won't keep watching. I never realized how boring I was until I looked back and compared my first videos to my later ones. No one wants a five-minute lead in on what you will be speaking about or why, they want to hear what you have to say as quickly as possible so that they can move on and watch the next video. You have to dive in on the topic you're speaking about, and cut out all the rest.

Dead air, or people struggling to find their words, equals boring, unprofessional vlogs that very few viewers will have the tolerance to watch. *You* may be willing to wait through your three-second pauses, because you know what you're about to say next, but my time is valuable as a viewer, and every empty moment feels like an hour. That means that you, as the vlogger, should not only edit your videos, but also rehearse what you want to say before you start filming. The more rehearsed you are, the more charismatic

you can attempt be.

Rule #1:

Don't Anger the Gods of Advertising!

Maybe this should have been the first lesson listed in this book; however, this is the golden rule of all monetized vlogs/blogs. If you are lucky enough to find sponsors, you then have to consider yourself an owned vlogger. If you conduct your posts in a way that displeases a sponsor, they will not hesitate to take their money elsewhere. So, what exactly does that mean for your vlog channel?

You'll likely need to give up swearing, if that's an issue. The occasional curse word is typically fine, but if you have the mouth of a sailor, you'll likely have great difficultly finding a company willing to attach their name to your product (in this situation, your personally made recordings would be your product). You will also have to kiss anything violent or sexual goodbye, as that is also not an image that most companies want to associate with. In addition, anything relating to copyrighted media, no matter how big or small of a part it plays in your posts, will usually get your sponsors to bail out on you as well.

Having said that, most of these problem areas are also gray areas that can be interpreted differently for every user. As an example, if you have videos of a karate tournament, the company sending you advertisements may decide that this is violent. The term "sexual" also doesn't apply to pornography, it can be as simple as filming a vlog while being wrapped up in a blanket (which qualifies as implied nudity). Even the set amount of profanity that a vlogger can use is unclear. As such, you may find yourself banned from sponsorship for using a single swear word, whereas other monetized vloggers might swear twice per sentence and continue to get paid. This may seem ridiculously anal when compared to some television media that always manages to find sponsors, but you, as the independent vlogger, are the little guy, and can be abused and exploited as such.

You would also be wise to familiarize yourself with the Freedom and Innovation Revitalizing United States Entrepreneurship Act of 2007, aka, the Fair Use Act. Essentially, "fair use" means that a vlogger can use copyrighted images, or small bits of music or video, if they are reviewing, criticizing, hosting a newscast, or otherwise explaining the material in their "show." With fair use, you do not need permission from the copyright holder to use their material in very small doses. The rules are vague and open for interpretation, though, and so, again, you can find yourself in trouble for doing something that another vlogger is getting away with.

Many advertising companies get accused of using unfair practices when enforcing what is and isn't allowed. Losing sponsorship happens regularly for small vloggers, and there is not much that they can do about it. Sometimes advertisers are removed even when the vlogger has done nothing wrong.

A close friend of mine recently experienced a horror story with her vlog's monetization, which came through the largest advertising company online, owned by the world's largest search engine (hint hint). At this moment, my vlog is still monetized with this company, so, for fear of my own income's safety, I will only refer to the advertising company as the-company-that-shall-not-be-named. But, to sum up their advertising basics, this company places commercials, as well as text ads, in your vlogs, and you get paid every time an add gets clicked by a viewer.

My friend, Jade, had been vlogging for several months; her videos had been monetized the entire time, and she had about 1,500 total views on her channel, which isn't a lot. She always used royalty free music in her videos, and everything else was her own original content. Since she never received a huge amount of traffic, she was quite stunned to be informed by the-company-that-shall-not-be-named that her monetization account was being permanently disabled.

Jade was given no cause for why this action was taken, except for a generic email stating that her account "posed a threat" to potentially generate invalid clicking activity on her advertisements. She had done nothing wrong. Even according to the email, no invalid clicks were detected, it was only stated that they could possibly happen in the future. The-company-that-shall-not-be-named refused to give her any further explanation as to why she was banned, had her current earnings forfeited, and could never make another penny from her own videos. There was no phone number to call, no real people to respond to her email inquiries for more information – nothing!

At that time, she had made only a few dollars, so the money wasn't too big of a deal. The real issue was that there had been no prior warnings, and now she could never again use this company to make money. The-company-that-shall-not-be-named claimed that they would be returning her earned revenue back to the advertisers (as she had somehow cheated them), even though the company continued to monetize her videos and keep that revenue for themselves. This is a strange action to take, since her earnings had been disabled under the accusation of having invalid click activity.

Jade filed the standard appeal to attempt to reclaim her account, but again, she was only sent another forum letter telling her to go away. The best the company ever told her was that their team of "specialists" confirmed that the decision to disable her account was valid, and that they can close any account, for any reason, at any time. They can also continue to post adds in anyone's videos and collect revenue for themselves, without having to share that money with the actual creator of the content.

Clearly, this is a group of tyrants that are abusing independent vloggers. If they had relevant information from real "specialists," there would be no issue with sharing this information with the disabled account holder. And, obviously, no one wants to consent to putting annoying advertisements in their videos for the sake of making someone else money. So, the vloggers that allow the services from the-company-that-shall-not-be-named are, quite frankly, getting screwed over. Sooner or later, this company disables most small-fry accounts before they have to pay the vlog owners.

Now that you are aware of this, be warned that, while monetization seems like a great, easy way to make money, it is also a slippery slope that can quickly change into a permanently burnt bridge. Jade did nothing wrong, her videos were not in violation of the company's terms of services, yet, the company has no interest in working with her, as they claim disabling her account is in "the best interest of the sponsors." The-company-that-shall-not-be-named is the judge, jury, and executioner, and Jade will likely never see a dime from her efforts as a monetized vlogger now.

So, if you do not like the idea of being creatively stifled, and/or allowing someone else to profit off of your work while you remain unpaid, then you should enter into monetization with extreme caution. Every company is out to make as much money as possible for themselves and their stockholders. They do not care about whether or not you're treated properly or ethically as the host site.

While you may think that you'll just monetize, then, rightfully, start a lawsuit against the-company-that-shall-not-be-named if such a thing ever happens to you, all I can say is good luck! Remember when the disgruntled employees of Wal-Mart tried to ban together and sue? The judge dismissed the case and told them that each person must file a separate case and fight the corporate mega-giant on an individual basis. The courts of the United States are set up for the wealthy companies who can afford a team of top attorneys; they will run you in circles, waste your time, and use every dirty tactic in the book to leave you empty handed, no matter how "right" you may be in the matter.

So, again, monetization is often more of a headache than it will ever be worth to a small, independent vlogger, and I recommend it only to advanced vloggers with thousands of loyal followers (who can flood the company with hate mail if your account is wrongfully disabled).

You Can Be Sabotaged!

After writing the last section, I feel it's only best to let everyone know that, if you have monetized your videos, you are in constant danger. Any time, for any reason, you can get a viewer who does not like you, and thereby "click bombs" your advertisements. A click bomb is repeatedly clicking on an ad, or ads, which makes the advertising company think that you have hired someone to fraudulently inflate your earnings.

In these situations, accounts are, unfortunately, disabled by the-company-that-shall-not-be-named rightfully, as multiple clicks on an ad are against your terms of service. It should still be pointed out, though, that there is a difference between purposefully clicking, or having others click, on your ads, and having someone spitefully click bomb your posts to sabotage your account. The latter is out of your control.

Now, why would someone click bomb you? Because they can! The Internet is full of psychos and people wanting to prove that they are somebody, and some people do that by taking their best attempt at ruining someone else's day/life/career/whatever. It could even be that you have an uninformed user who is clicking your ads in the hopes of helping you earn more revenue because they like you. For whatever reason(s), click bombing happens, and the vloggers have little to no recourse in the aftermath.

Instead of banning the click bomber, advertising companies, such as the-company-that-shall-not-be-named, will blame you, disable your account, and you'll never see the money that you earned honestly. This is a completely backwards business model for advertising companies, as, in the real world, if you're fired on a Friday morning, they still have to pay you for Monday through Thursday. As a vlogger, you are abused and told that all of your work is invalid, and so no paycheck will ever be given to you.

It can also be the case that the-company-that-shall-not-be-named sabotaged you to avoid paying you. Search online, and you will find endless stories about people who had anywhere from one dollar to ten thousand dollars in their account, and then they log in one day to find that their account was disabled under a, supposedly, made-up cause. This company may also say that your account has the "potential" to do wrong, and thereby disable your account simply due to suspicion (as with what happened with Jade). Again, there is no recourse when this happens, as the-company-that-shall-not-be-named reserves the right (I wonder whether this "right" is legal) to terminate anyone's service for any reason, and keep their earnings.

The claimed cause for revoking the user's pay is that the-company-that-shall-not-be-named turns around and refunds the paying sponsors for the fraudulent click(s). However, as a former paying advertiser of the-company-that-shall-not-be-named, I reported several fraudulent clicks that I had received on my advertisement campaign. Not only did I never see one red cent credited to my account, but the company never responded to my complaints either. How a giant corporation can avoid paying their users can only reflect on the evils of Capitalism in America that need to be put back into balance.

If you are disabled by the-company-that-shall-not-be-named, you have several other monetization options that you can research online. However, none will produce the same mount of revenue, and may involve removing your videos for the most popular video hosting websites online. Sine the other options are less popular, it's unlikely that you'll find financial success easily.

Even with monetization aside, you can still run the risk of getting your videos "flagged," or reported, by viewers. This report then goes to the website hosting your video, and their staff reviews your content. At this point, you are at the mercy of a nameless employee, who is of an unknown moral character, and who may or may not delete your video on a whim. I recommend saving copies of all of your videos in case you find yourself in the need to take them from Host Site A to Host Site B at a later date.

Copyrights Run Both Ways

Copyright and trademark laws are probably the single biggest source of frustration for a vlogger. While, on the one hand, some companies may be pleased that you give an unprompted shout out to their products (since it is free advertising and all), many others may not want to be a part of your video. Because of this, you, as a vlogger, have to be constantly aware of what you are sharing in your videos, if it can be considered piracy, or if it constitutes copyright infringement versus fair use. Again, this is another gray area, where it seems that some vloggers can get away with doing anything, and others get their videos deleted for upsetting a copyright owner.

There also comes the issue of whether or not to copy protect your own, original creations, so that you can prevent theft. As an artistic person, or even a wannabe public figure, the threat of having your original ideas and talents stolen is very frightening. There is nothing worse than working hard on creating a song, or sharing an idea for a film or book, and then find out that someone else has swooped in, stolen your idea, and made a profit from it without even giving you proper credit.

Many vloggers have thought that the idea of copyrighting or trademarking their Internet creations is laughable. Often times, it is, and there are certain things that most people don't even have the ability to copyright. For instance, you would find it difficult to copyright a video of yourself commenting on clips from films, because the clips are already copyrighted property of the studio. You could, however, copyright a video where you made your grandmother's secret recipe for buffalo sauce (provided that you use generic ingredients and/or do not disclose specific brand names).

However, when you create logos, music, photos, ideas, and the like, it is all your property, so it is up to you to decide whether or not it's worth protecting. Simply posting a video online does not prove that you thought of it first. Neither does the poor man's copyright, where you write something down, mail it to yourself, and leave the envelope sealed (to show a type of copyright date with the postmark on the stamp). These types of ownership rarely hold up in court, and the only way to truly win, should you ever find a need to enter into litigation, is to have a government form showing you as the copyright/trademark/patent/etc holder, and that form must be dated before the documentation of the person that you believe has stolen from you.

    I recommend keeping anything particularly important or original "steal proof" in this way. You may find it flattering if you write a song and a thousand other people cover that song in their own videos; but, what if a record label uses the song, or sells it internationally? Even the vloggers creating their own cover could be earning revenue off of your creation. I can't speak for everyone, but I would not be okay with that.

Now, while you all laugh and say this will never apply to you, all I can say in my defense is that you never know. Sure, the average vlogger has no real danger of being threatened or ripped off, but, then again, you can't tell what will become popular online. While most vloggers will never go viral, you may wake up one day, after decades of vlogging, and find that you suddenly have millions of hits on a single video. So, my repeated message from this book is to be paranoid and prepared rather than get caught with your pants down.

Be You...

But More Interesting

Most people start vlogging because they have something to talk about. Whether that be about their crappy job, their crazy kids, how hot they think they are, or even to fill the Internet with tutorial knowledge, there is some driving factor that gets a person to start recording. Whatever your reasons for vlogging are, be certain that you are ready to present yourself to the world.

I am almost mortified to watch my first six months of vlogs. They are slow, unedited, and, quite simply put, boring. I have no flavor, no personality, no sense of fun in what I'm doing.

Instead, I speak to the camera like a teacher who is worn out from years of bratty students, and is timidly calling out to see if anyone even cares about what she has to say any longer. That's not me.

At least, not the "me" that I wanted to be presenting to my viewers. I had to find a way to bring out the entertaining character that my friends knew and, sometimes, liked. When I figured out how to do that, my subscriptions went from four (yes, just 4) to over two hundred. I let go of my inhibitions and allowed a more perky, fun, opinionated, and animated girl loose.

Every vlogger needs a persona; a go-to set of behaviors for when you are "on." Whether that persona be a squeaky clean role model, a punk rocker, or even a mental patient, you have to develop yourself to be both interesting and entertaining to watch. This isn't something that you will likely create, or master, in a day, but, just as you can pick and choose what viewers are allowed to see in your recordings, you can also pick and choose whoever you want to be.

Be Interesting, Not Ashamed

If you are self-conscious about anything, it will present itself, exponentially, on film. If you're homosexual and pretending not to be in your vlogs, people will start to notice, and then they usually start to call you names. If you hold yourself back because you're embarrassed about your weight, or because your ears stick out, or you don't like your voice, that will also become obvious in your mannerisms, and, again, people will ridicule you for it.

I've been a photographer for years, and I cannot tell you how often personal issues show up on someone's face and in their body language.

I've had beautiful, young ladies give me forced, sheepish smiles because they feel insecure about their size. They don't believe they're pretty, and, even though they don't openly disclose that to me, it becomes obvious in how they conduct themselves around me.

As badly as insecurities show up in photographs, they come through a thousand times more prominent in a recording. So, if you are struggling with issues about who you are or want to be, everyone else will see that, even if you don't say a word about it. They may not be able to pinpoint exactly what you don't like about yourself, or what you might be trying to hide, but the audience will always pick up that something is off about you. And, unfortunately, many people over the Internet are not kind or forgiving for any issues that you may have. If you can't resolve your issues before filming, do not post public vlogs!

My suggestion is to own who you are, simply because, if you own yourself, than no one else can. If you feel that you are heavier than the average person, than announce that in your first video without shame or remorse. Then, if some nasty spirited hater calls you a "fatty" six months later, you've already owned that fact publicly and can tell them as much.

I've had several occasions where someone told me that my make-up looked like crap. I have already proclaimed that I am a "non-make-up artist" who has lightly studied the craft, and that

I was certain that a real cosmetologist could point out a million flaws in my make-up applications. So, when these people gave me a negative comment I would retort that "no, it's not crap it's ____ brand!" and go about my day.

However, I do not recommend stating things to try to excuse who you are. Using the size issue as an example again, if you claim that you're overweight, but you really want to lose weight and are trying, then you find a whole new load of trouble for yourself. That tells viewers that you are ashamed of yourself, and it may additionally imply that you want to change to suit their tastes. This gives trolls some fodder later on to try and kick up drama to hurt your feelings.

A hater may decide to start harassing you months later, announcing that you must not be trying to lose weight too hard, because you're still just as hefty. Believe me, that kind of personal attack will hit you much harder than you think. The blow is easier to deal with if you've already started out with the demeanor of "I'm fat, so what?"

Even if you don't find it necessary to make that statement in a vlog post, you need to think it privately – and believe it! Your attitude about yourself says it all, so be truly you, and proud to be just that. No apologies, no shame. If the viewers don't like it, they can move right along to the next video!

Inconsistency = Haters.

Consistency = Haters.

If you are a three-dimensional person, who has multiple interests, and constantly changes things around, some people will hate you for that. If you are a one-dimensional person, who always talks about the same subjects and behaves identically from one post to the next, some people will hate you for that too. After a lot of trial and error, I came to realize that, no matter what I did or how I behaved, I would never be able to please everyone.

This is one of the most important lessons for anyone who is putting themselves into a public environment to learn; especially online, where users often get brave and say mean things that they would never say to your face. If you do not have thick skin, vlogging is not for you! Eventually, trolls will pick on everything about you. Once you go public, every detail becomes fair game: hair, eyes, nose, teeth, skin, body, voice, opinions, beliefs, intelligence, heck, even your children aren't off limits!

There have been times where I received extreme praise, and it made my day. However, those pleasant comments are easily forgotten when someone makes fun of your flaws (or tries to make them up). Once, I was attacked for having "crappy sound" - except that, "crappy" is the much more polite version of what this user posted for all to read. It got under my skin, badly, so I gave him some nasty comments back, reminding the user that this was a free tutorial, and that they were welcome to go pay for a book instead. Sometimes I don't get why people choose to comment so often when they don't like you. Why not just leave the page and move on to the next video?

Even more frustrating are those who leave "thumbs down" ratings with no explanation as to why. You are unable to track which users rate your videos on most hosting sites, so it's hard to even know if people genuinely dislike your posts, or if you have a few haters who are constantly being passive aggressive towards your work. Either way, though, it hurts to be aware that people don't like you. So, if you are the least bit insecure, or let those types of comments shake you up, you will find vlogging to be more stressful than rewarding.

As for myself, as much as I dislike being disliked, I consider myself to be pretty tough. I don't generally allow anyone to chase me off of my turf, and, so, at times, I find myself stirring the pot to make trouble, just to prove that I can take whatever the haters can dish out. Being a vlogger is very similar to being an actor, in that, we tend to be a group that thrives on attention and hates rejection. Be sure that you can handle both ends of this spectrum before entering into vlogging, and, if you find that it's too much for you, there is no shame in admitting that and stopping further posts, or deleting old ones.

However, if you are lucky enough to be able to thrive on conflict and/or negative energy, you will likely find a wonderful and fulfilling experience posting online. Use the negative energy to your advantage! Vlog about it, ridicule the users who hate on you, take the higher road and keep vlogging in spite of them, or even use their mean words as an excuse to tease yourself and claim their power. While it does take time to adjust to receiving nasty comments on a daily basis, haters should eventually bring you up and fuel you, not rip out your emotions.

If you're unsure of whether or not you can adapt to do this, please stay away from being a public figure. You have to always be able to brush it off and carry on vlogging for your own reasons. If a troll notices that they are upsetting you, a horde of haters will start to attack without cause – and it never ends!

When in Doubt; Fake It!

Some of the people who vlog are experts in their field; others are not so qualified in a real-world sense. Maybe you are seeking a video on how to fix your gaming console. You might find videos created by technicians with fifty years of experience, but, realistically, those people will be working for a salary somewhere – not posting videos online.

While some professionals are posting vlogs, and making a living at it, you have to remember that most trained and experienced pros have no desire to make videos to help others for free. So, more than likely, you will find a lot of younger people offering up free tutorials on how to fix your console system. That doesn't mean they're bad, or wrong, it just means that you will have to proceed with caution when trying to perform these actions yourself.

Similarly, there are millions of young girls who decide to create make-up related vlog channels. They may get thousands of subscribers and fans, yet have never been to any cosmetology school to have the "authority" to teach anyone anything. All the same, people tune in to hear what they have to say and see what they're doing.

The lesson to pull from this is that you can vlog about anything without having to be a certified expert. Personally, I made many tutorials for animation while in my first semester of animation classes. In the beginning, I did this so that I could have a reference for myself to look back on. However, due to hard drive space limitations, I ended up slapping an Animatimon logo in the front of the videos and posting them online so that I could remove them from my computer. These vlogs are among my most popular, and they help other people. I am in no way qualified to teach animation, but I was more than capable of regurgitating what I had learned, as I was learning it. So, even if you don't know everything you're talking about inside and out, you can still vlog about it and help people all the same.

Don't Vlog With Friends!

You and your buddy think that vlogging is the greatest thing in the world, and so you want to vlog together. Why not? After all, it seems like a great way to get attention, spread your knowledge and opinions, and, maybe, even get paid! That was our intention when starting 2 Geek Girls, and, having known each other for over a decade, we were confident in what to expect from one another. You may not be as lucky.

Just think... After a few months, your vlogging venture starts to go south. Your friend thinks that they did most of the work on the videos; they thought of the idea, made up the topics, bought the computer or camera, and did all of the editing and uploading.

If you have a monetized vlog that is making you some money, your friend may start to believe that they deserve a bigger cut than you because you do less work. Even without money being involved, they may decide that they want to quit altogether and leave you high and dry. Then what?

It happens with many young vloggers, where they get into an argument and stop being friends with someone. Before long, the former friend demands to be removed from all of the videos. Or, even worse, a group of minors decide to record and post their vlogs, and later the parents find out and do not like the project.

Before we go any farther, let me stress this point to anyone under eighteen: *if you're a minor, you should never vlog with anyone else,* **and** *make sure that your parents approve of what you're doing in the first place as a vlogger.* If your parents are divorced, you legally have to have both of them consent to your vlog. The same is also true if your parents are still married, but they are less likely to fight one another in a disagreement. Just an FYI though, Dad or Mom can get your vlog taken down in a heartbeat, and you have no say-so as a minor.

I began making websites in 1997, long before vlogs were even in existence. Even though I was fourteen, my mother would flip her top if she found a photo of me posted online. The idea of her being that overprotective was maddening to me; I could not understand why she insisted on being so uptight over the personal pride that I felt in my design work. But, when your options are removing the picture, or having your mother calling the service provider to take down your website, you get backed into a corner. While you may think that you'll protest and rebel, you will not win against a diligent and angry parent, so don't even try it. Legally speaking, no one can enter into a contract with a minor anyways, and, as such, minors are not allowed to enter into agreements with most web services to begin with – so, don't press your luck if you're underage.

Now, going back to vlogging with friends. Paperwork is your true best friend - not your flesh and blood friends. If you are making a documentary and want your friends to be in it, have them sign release forms. If you want to partner up with your friends and make a web show, get a contract signed and validated that outlines what each of you want and expect from working together (who gets paid what, responsibilities, work times, number of episodes, what happens if someone doesn't meet their responsibilities, etc).

Contracts work, because, at one point, you may want to fire Friend A, because they never show up to film, and you want to replace them with Friend B. But, Friend A can freak out and say that the show was their idea and you're stealing their intellectual property. Then the show never happens, and you have all wasted your efforts. So, while it may seem ridiculous to enter into a legal agreement with your BFF, it is much safer for everyone involved to cover your rears from the start.

You can find generic release forms and contracts all over the Internet. But, please don't ever forget that no one is able to enter into a contract with a minor, and it is considered child pornography in many states to record or photograph minors without their parent's consent and/or presence. Yes, this is true even if you are all clothed and behave like angels the entire time you're on camera. And with today's lawsuit-happy world, not adhering to these laws can get you in a big pile of problems down the road.

In the case of a co-hosted web show, it is also not a bad idea to get an EIN (employer identification number) if you start making money. The EINs are given out by the government, for free, and will allow you to become a new business entity. You will not only be allowed to open bank accounts in the name of the web series, but you may find certain tax benefits to this as well (depending on your earnings, location, etc). Most web shows will not need or require an EIN, though; this is just a topic to think about with your partner if you are seeking long term and financial goals.

Social Media is your BFF

There seems to be a dozen new social networking sites popping up everyday. Some are very generalized, featuring billions of users, and have mobile app counterparts. Others may be smaller and focus on a particular subject matter. Your job is to find the best ones; the most popular ones; and the ones that you are the most comfortable with, to use and exploit to draw attention to your product – which would be your vlog channel.

The best rule to follow for this is that there are no rules. You can have your own social media profile on several different networks, and you will gain different followers for each one. Some vloggers have their videos auto-posted to their social media pages, others like to personalize it more by announcing their new vlogs, and others still will promote the same video several times a day in the hopes of getting new people to notice the vlog. Since most social networking pages are free to create and use, it's a fantastic, and economical, way to advertise that you exist.

Another tactic for social media advertising is to find pages and groups that feature similar content to your product. For example, if you are vlogging about candy, you may go to all the major candy profile pages and post your vlog there. Be forewarned though, while many larger companies won't notice these posts (because hundreds of people post every hour), you still run the risk of getting flagged as spam, having your posts deleted by admins, and/or getting your account closed down for appearing to be a nuisance. With that in mind, tread lightly and do not over post your videos.

The process of tagging another profile in your status update also has the same potential for going wrong. However, tagging is less likely to be reported. On many social networking sites, if you start typing in the name of the other page, tagging options will automatically appear. With other sites, you will have to know the exact username of the page to tag them properly. Again, this will get easier as you familiarize yourself with posting on these sites.

Many social pages also feature thousands of online communities for vloggers. This can prove to be an amazing resource for tips and ideas. Mom vloggers, work at home vloggers, business vloggers, techie vloggers, media vloggers, there is a fan page/group for every genre out there! Those groups of users may even be willing to answer your questions, give you advice, or help you through rough patches. But, you'll never know what's out there if you don't go looking, and there is no definitive way to find out which groups will be beneficial to you until you try them out. So, don't be shy, and network yourself with every free minute that you have available.

Who Do You Vlog For?

My favorite lesson in vlogging is to figure out exactly who or what you are working for. Many people feel like they are working for money, or a particular fan base (military spouses, moms, techno-nuts, gamers, etc). Some even feel like they are vlogging for the sake of their sponsors as they attempt to do a delicate dance to keep everyone happy. None of these answers are right, though, and will likely end up putting you into a miserable state at one point or another.

You have to have the drive and desire to vlog, simply because you want to. Most vloggers never become famous, make money, or get viewers. Yet they keep recording. Why? Because the process of creating and sharing is done for themselves; it's an outlet for them to release, be a character, feel important, or even let off steam. You should vlog because you love doing it, then see what comes your way in the future.

If you get carried away and start obsessing over getting a certain number of viewers, fans, subscribers, or whatever else, you will be chasing unimportant goals. What is important is that you are an individual with a voice, and that you have decided to stand up and express that to whoever is willing to watch or listen. This ideology applies to so many areas of life: do what makes you happy and drives you forward, talk about what you are passionate about, and don't let anyone else define who you are.

Ending Thoughts

At this time, now that you have, undoubtedly, clung desperately onto my every word, I would like the take a moment to be gracious and thank my readers. I am grateful to everyone who purchases a copy of this book. By purchasing this book, you are helping to put an end to Liberal Studies post-graduation poverty. And, for my final kernel of wisdom, I will tell you all this:

If you go to college, you would be well advised to enter into a degree program in a field that is full of gainful employment. This could include areas such as medical jobs, mathematics, engineering, and the sciences. If you decide to go into Liberal Studies, Film, English (non-teaching), or other arts or humanity fields, you may very well find yourself unemployable, with large student loan debt, trying to piece together poorly-conceived book ideas to make a living.

With much love to all of you for reading:
Megan Gotham
Vlogger,
Blogger,
Producer,
Director,
Editor,
Developer,
Consultant,
Artistic Director,
Actor/Personality,
Writer,
Publisher,
Perpetual Student,
Geek,
& Mom, Wife, and Friend

www.ingramcontent.com/pod-product-compliance
Lightning Source LLC
Chambersburg PA
CBHW030904180526
45163CB00004B/1704